MEDITATIONS
FOR THE
LATER YEARS

MEDITATIONS FOR THE LATER YEARS

Josephine Robertson

Drawings by Giorgetta Bell McRee

ABINGDON PRESS
Nashville • *New York*

MEDITATIONS FOR THE LATER YEARS

Copyright © 1974 by Abingdon Press

All rights in this book are reserved.
No part of the book may be reproduced in any manner whatsoever without written permission of the publishers except brief quotations embodied in critical articles or reviews. For information address Abingdon Press, Nashville, Tennessee.

Library of Congress Cataloging in Publication Data

ROBERTSON, JOSEPHINE.
   Meditations for the later years.

   1. Aged—Prayer-books and devotions—English.
I. Title.
BV4580.R57   242'.6'5   73-19935

ISBN 0-687-24099-9

MANUFACTURED BY THE PARTHENON PRESS AT
NASHVILLE, TENNESSEE, UNITED STATES OF AMERICA

with loving appreciation to my sisters,
Mary Helen and Carolyn

PREFACE

When we discuss the later years, we must recognize the difference between the retiree who travels, gardens, and takes an active role in the community and the person, unable to share in such activities, who may be confined to a nursing home. These thoughts for the bonus years, for the most part, concern those who still have many options, but I hope there will be some encouragement, too, for those whose choices have narrowed. The question is basically the same for both: "How may I live most fully the life I have?"

Josephine Robertson
Boulder, Colorado

CONTENTS

1. The Bonus Years . 13
2. Chinooks . 15
3. What Is a Home? . 17
4. The Extra Dimension . 20
5. This Is the Day . 22
6. A Bag with Holes . 25
7. Wayside Shrines . 27
8. Memorials . 29
9. A New View of Hospitals . 31
10. Too Much Solitaire . 33
11. Bells . 35
12. Understanding . 38
13. Compensations . 40
14. Two Sides of the Road . 42
15. Harmony . 44
16. The Box of Wilted Flowers . 47
17. Sharing Now . 49
18. Retirement Incentives . 51
19. The Cross in the Workshop . 53
20. When Worry Gnaws . 56

21. *A Time to Speak—and How* . 58
22. *Caring* . 60
23. *The Perfect Tribute* . 62
24. *Have a Good Day* . 64
25. *Trees Without Leaves* . 66
26. *Thanksgiving* . 69
27. *The Quiet Moments of Christmas* . 71
28. *Breaking New Ground—*
A Thought for the New Year . 74
29. *Enlarge Our Love* . 76
30. *The Time Is Now* . 78

THE BONUS YEARS

Dost thou love life? then do not squander time, for that is the stuff life is made of. Benjamin Franklin

Retirement is a surprisingly new idea. In earlier times men worked as long as they were able or until their sons took over or until their savings permitted them to stop. The idea of a vacation never occurred to my own grandparents or to many others. Leisure presented few problems. Today, with mandatory retirement in most fields of work, we come to the cutoff date—ready or not. There is a sort of legend that the presentation of the symbolic watch is almost as traumatic as the arrival of a priest to administer last rites. But it need not be this way.

Ahead are the bonus years for men and women with reasonably good health, Medicare to cushion illness, and an assured, if modest, income. The retiree is like the student who has completed the required courses and now can choose some interesting electives.

Freedom *not* to work is sufficient for some. Travel is the first thought for many, but the weeks on the road pass quickly and in coming home, the main problem is waiting on the doorstep. Others grope for something meaningful. Now one ponders these questions: What would I like to accomplish? What would I like to learn? How can I help?

The answers do not come all at once. This is the time for watching and for having a receptive spirit. Small opportunities welcomed can lead to more satisfying ones in recreation, education, community service, and in our churches. How can we best enrich the life we have?

Our Father, we thank thee for these years of opportunity. Show us the way to use them well and in thy service.

CHINOOKS

Dost thou know the balancings of the clouds, the wondrous works of him which is perfect in knowledge?   Job 37:16

    Sometimes in our mountain country, on a day which starts with biting cold, we will feel a sudden, warm wind which may send the mercury up as much as thirty degrees. The change seems incredible, but as the chinook, or "snow eater," floods us with warmth, we forget about the cold. While many scientific studies have been made of this phenomenon, those of us who are nonscientific, like the poet of the Old Testament, marvel at the mysterious "balancings of the clouds."
    We all know people who like the "snow eaters" can enter our lives with flooding warmth. I think of a child who skips into a room trailing joy, a clergyman whose interest in others is so vital that drooping spirits are

freshened, a recreation director in a nursing home who brightens every room she enters. I think of friends in whose companionship we can always laugh and find renewal. I think of Christ, who could break through defensive barriers with pervasive radiance.

Admittedly, we are not all endowed with charismatic personalities, but we can grow in our capacity to thaw the cold in other lives by following some simple lines of action. We can show we care by not talking about ourselves, but by asking questions and listening. We can do the unexpected, especially remembering significant days and dates. We can seek opportunities to praise and compliment. We can look for shared interests.

It seems a near miracle when on a cold, raw day, a warm wind makes it balmy. As we have experienced such changes in our own hearts, so God willing, we can bring warmth to others.

Help us, our Father, to be sensitive to the needs of others and to be channels of their joy.

WHAT IS A HOME?

Every house where love abides and friendship is a guest,
Is surely home and home sweet home; for there the heart can rest.   *Henry Van Dyke*

Because of his work the couple traveled and lived all over the world, but the wife did not regard this as a hardship. "As soon as we're in a new place, it's our home and we become involved. I offer myself as a volunteer."

Home used to be a fixed point and our grandparents were apt to stay in theirs all their lives. "The old home place" was a fact, not a wistful sentiment. With the swing from an agricultural to an industrial society, employee moves have become commonplace, more painful for the family than for the busy and ambitious father. Often the first transfer is the

hardest when wife and children find themselves suddenly not only without friends, but without their interested doctor, pastor, grocer,

(18)

and garage mechanic. However, good friends are not lost through distance, and there are new friends to be made. Adjustments become easier with experience. Consequently in the later years, people who have moved around find change easier than those pulling up roots for the first time. The experienced do not use the term "back home." Home has moved with them.

Home no longer means only a house with a front yard. It can be an apartment, a town house, or a single room in a retirement residence—any of which can be changed from a motel-like sterility to a warm, hospitable place with a few personal pictures, books, mementoes, and a kettle ready to prepare a welcoming hot drink for the visitor. Home is an atmosphere, a spirit, and it can be ours, just as the presence of God can be ours, wherever our destiny takes us.

Help us, we pray, while cherishing memories of past joys, to live fully and warmly the experiences and opportunities of today.

THE EXTRA DIMENSION

Fear thou not; for I am with thee. I will strengthen thee.   Isaiah 41:10

Something was wrong with the plane. Unfinished breakfast trays were whisked away abruptly, and then word came from the captain. There would be an emergency landing and the hostesses would give instructions. The girls took away eyeglasses, purses, anything sharp or hard. They brought pillows and showed how to lean forward and cushion the head. Meanwhile the plane was circling, dumping gas. As it lost altitude, firetrucks and ambulances were visible below. How did the passengers feel? One of them told me. "There was no panic. Everyone was very quiet. I prayed, then checked back in my mind, glad that I had left my affairs in order at home. I prayed some more, and it seemed as though we entered another dimension of living, as though we were experiencing a strength and courage far beyond normal. The critical moment came. Our pilot made the landing safely, and we all cheered." But there were also silent prayers of thanks.

At some time most of us have known that extra dimension. It might be in the familiar situation of overwhelming stage fright and then going out to speak to an audience with complete composure. It may have been in a fire or accident when panic was supplanted with clearheaded action. It may have been in the acceptance of tragic news when instead of collapse, a sudden flow of strength made the next steps possible or in a flooding sense of peace before critical surgery. In times like these we know there is a strength beyond our own, for "I am with thee."

We thank thee, God, for resources beyond our understanding. Replace our fear with faith and make us receptive to the inflow of thy transcendent spirit.

THIS IS THE DAY

This is the day which the Lord hath made; we will rejoice and be glad in it.   Psalm 118:24

Sometimes we have days which we wish the Lord *hadn't* made, days when things go wrong, when energy runs low, when physical aches and old griefs recur. Far from rejoicing, we can identify better with the psalmist's cry of despair, "The waters are come into my soul." There is no pushbutton cure for these dark days, but there is a variety of simple procedures, some of which may help.

We can stress the thought that even if the problems persist, tomorrow may be one of the good days when we can cope with life.

We can accept this day as a loss, take a nap, and keep away from others whom we might depress.

We can summon up our dramatic ability

to act as if everything was fine. This is kind to our associates, even if they are not fooled.

We can set ourselves a project of accomplishing or making something as simple as a tool rack or an apron, remembering how beatific our children used to become when they had created something with their own hands.

We can lose ourselves in a book or drama, hoping it will furnish emotional catharsis.

We can ease tension with physical exercise.

We can go where other people are, deliberately entering into discussions and activities—thereby possibly emerging from our private darkness.

We can pray, not focusing on our depression but giving thanks for everything we can think of that is good in our lives.

The psalmist says firmly "We will rejoice and be glad in it." It may not be that simple, but we can make a good try.

We pray that as the sun can send long shafts of light through broken clouds, so may the light of thy spirit renew our joy in the life thou hast given us.

A BAG WITH HOLES

He that earneth wages, earneth wages to put it into a bag with holes.   Haggai 1:6

Although this graphic and rueful picture dates back some twenty-five hundred years, it has a modern ring—particularly around income tax time. Our wages, earned from work in past years, often seem to go into a bag of many holes—some of which we have caused and others that are beyond our control. Haggai's concern was that his people were frittering away their resources while they might better set about rebuilding the temple.

Anyone who has put a son or daughter on a strict allowance remembers that first reaction of glorious freedom when a week's allotment for school lunches might go into two magnificent banana splits or a month's clothing allowance on a flamboyant jacket, leaving nothing for shoes. It takes experience to be aware of the holes in the bag, and some of us are a long time learning.

With incomes reduced in retirement, we still have choices. We can spend everything on ourselves, or we can cut down on some items and figure where we would most like to help. It might be the "adoption" of an orphan through a relief agency, nature conservation, minority education, medical research, or some special outreach of our religious body. All these things put beliefs into action beyond the limited orbit of our own lives. While our particular church may be in excellent condition, we may well take the advice of the venerable prophet—stop wasting our assets and get on with the "building of the temple."

Help us, we pray, to reach beyond our own immediate wishes and comforts and share in the building of a better world in the spirit of Christ.

WAYSIDE SHRINES

Where cross the crowded ways of life . . .
We hear Thy voice, O Son of Man.
Frank Mason North

There was a charming colored chromo in a walnut frame on the wall of the room where I slept when I visited my grandparents' home on the Iowa bank of the Mississippi. The picture showed two children kneeling at a wayside shrine along a tree shaded country road. I have wondered since how this found its way into that strict Scotch Presbyterian home, but I admired it and wished we could do things like that instead of going to our unromantic Sunday school in the musty "church parlor."

Wayside shrines may still be found in our country in the southwest where the Catholic traditions of Mexico have inspired the devout to build them in gratitude for prayers answered. They are used by other worshipers who may never know the names of their builders, but who appreciate this particular way of offering thanks.

Wayside shrines, so appropriate for country roads where travelers could pause as they rested their feet or their horses, no longer fit into a country of expressways and diverse religions. Yet we, too, can worship as we go. We can slip into a quiet church for a moment —yes on a weekday. There are chapels in many airports and hospitals that are truly urban wayside shrines. But we need neither shrines nor altars nor buildings to worship as we travel the road of everyday life. A quick prayer for courage, understanding, or guidance known only to God can be our equivalent to kneeling at a wayside shrine, and helping others can be our thanks offering.

Help us, we pray, to weave our faith and gratitude into the fabric of our daily living.

MEMORIALS

Far off thou art, but ever nigh;
I have thee still, and I rejoice . . .
I shall not lose thee though I die.
                    Alfred, Lord Tennyson

Every year a distinguished professor contributed chancel flowers in memory of his wife. When he was asked if his regular Sunday was her birthday or the day of her death, he said no. It commemorated the "asking day," the day he had asked her to marry him and she had accepted, a milestone day of happiness.

On another Sunday there was an exquisite arrangement of pink rosebuds and white daisies, and in the bulletin appeared the note, "Today's flowers are given in joyous memory of our little daughter." The heartbreaking blow had been accepted and the grief fully experienced, and in time the memory of the radiant child came clear again.

Again I am reminded of the inscriptions on beautifully situated benches in Kew Gardens "in happy memory of——" persons we never knew, but whose memories were honored with joy.

We share the companionship of different people along life's road. The "best friends" of our childhood drift away. Usually our parents go ahead of us, leaving tender memories. The husbands, wives, children, close friends—so much a part of our happiness—may leave us, causing our deepest grief. Only God goes the whole way with us. For the bereft there is a fork in the road. One way follows the path of bitterness. "Why does such a cruel thing happen?" The other is the path of acceptance. "I don't know why this blow should fall, but I know my life has been blessed by this love, and I will remember it with gratitude and joy."

We thank thee that thou art always with us. Give us the faith to accept loss, to trust in the face of mystery, and to remember with gratitude.

A NEW VIEW OF HOSPITALS

And Jesus went about . . . healing all manner of sickness.   Matt. 4:23

    For those of us not in the medical profession a hospital may be a place to hurry past. We associate it with anxious days for ourselves or our relatives. It seems very different now that I am working a few hours a week as a volunteer. I find a surprising sense of joy in a hospital. Doctors, nurses, therapists hurry past leaving a trail of purpose and enthusiasm, for they are using their skills to the fullest. Near the information desk where I am a hostess, I can hear the admitting clerk talking with people coming in for surgery. She is so kind and so interested that sometimes former patients stop by to thank her for lightening their low moments. The physical therapists are so bright and encouraging that the handicapped must feel better just for their presence. Perhaps because this is a church-sponsored hospital, the nurses show special concern. The chaplain comes to offer a prayer for each patient on the morning of surgery.

There are moments to treasure such as the young man coming from obstetrics to tell his friends, "We have a boy!" His face was shining with wonder and awe as if such a thing had never happened before.

In our busier hospitals there are opportunities for many kinds of volunteer service, and I notice that many of my coworkers are of retirement age. I notice, too, that we look forward to our weekly morning, afternoon, or evening. Our role is a modest one, but in a hospital where Christ's work of healing is carried on, we help by freeing the experts of detail—and in the course of our work we experience some of the drama of human life.

We thank thee for hospitals where lives begin and end and where ills are alleviated by a dedicated staff. We thank thee for their compassion and their joy in healing.

TOO MUCH SOLITAIRE

People are lonely because they build walls instead of bridges.   Joseph Fort Newton

A man who lived alone and seemed to have few friends died in the apartment house where we once lived. When a neighbor went in to help take care of his belongings, she was struck by a strange thing. His main interest must have been solitaire! All around were cards, game books, and diagrams—surely a lonely way to pass the time. It seemed symbolic of the isolated person who either could not or would not reach out to make contact with others.

Read any article about the elderly and the word loneliness is almost sure to appear in the first paragraph—and for obvious reasons. Members of our family die, our children move away, our good friends are scattered from

Florida to heaven. Since not many people are seeking us out at this point, our choice is between an ever shrinking circle or an active effort to widen it.

When we are much alone, we focus on ourselves and tend to lose our sensitivity to others. We lose the habit of laughter, the stimulus of exchanging ideas, forget the hunger of others for friendship, and so have less to offer.

Now is the time to search out new contacts, even if it means going alone to meetings of strangers. Those with special hobbies can attend gatherings ranging from bird watching to genealogy. Those craving sociability can go to senior centers or meetings for retired persons. If in a new community, search out a congenial church and watch for opportunities to volunteer. In our later years, bridge building is an important activity.

Help us, we pray, to make the effort to find shared interests and new channels of service.

BELLS

Iron bells!
What a world of solemn thought their melody
*   compels!   Edgar Allan Poe*

   We were strolling through an old cathedral town in England on a Sunday afternoon, a golden September day, when the great bells began to ring out. Called by their voices, we left the monastery ruins, the gardens brilliant with late summer bloom, and found a bench in the shadow of the ancient building. Changes were rung as well as old familiar hymns. So deep and rich were the tones that we not only heard but felt their vibrations. For an hour we were immersed in the flood of religious music from the venerable bells.
   For many of us bells were a part of our childhood. We heard the schoolbell, the town clock that struck the hour, and the bells sum-

moning the faithful to Sunday school, mass, or Protestant services. Sometimes there was the tolling of a funeral bell. We knew the voice of each church—Presbyterian, Methodist, Catholic, and the little church that had only an old locomotive bell. In many places the bells no longer ring. People living close by call for noise abatement. The bell for our present church was pulled across the plains by oxcart a century ago, but now silent, it stands on a pedestal with a suitable inscription. In our urban society, the bell is no longer the voice of the church.

But when occasionally we once again hear the ringing, it is like meeting an old friend who brings back a flood of memories. We remember those straight pews, our first teachers and preachers who dedicated themselves to starting us off with a set of values for living. We can be grateful that they cared. Perhaps their teachings would not exactly fit our specific needs today, even as the role of the bells has changed—but how nobly they both served their purpose!

We thank thee for the music of our faith. May it always sing in our hearts.

UNDERSTANDING

Kindness is the golden chain by which society is bound together.   Goethe

She was only five, but motherly in her relation to her younger brother.

"Johnny can't keep secrets," she confided. "He always tells me what's in his present for me."

"Well, after all, Johnny's really too little to keep secrets."

"Yes, I know," she nodded gravely. "So I just forget."

If we could achieve this level of understanding in our relationships, how much happier we would be! We would accept the quirks and frailties of others as part of the package and not let these be a barrier to companionship. Neither we nor our friends are perfect, nor were those with whom Christ associated, but he looked beyond their faults.

Today's clergymen, unlike employers who can give notice to individuals who don't measure up, must work with the whole person. He knows that Mr. A is critical of the missions, Mrs. B thinks the youth program too radical, Mr. C has a problem with alcohol, Mrs. D is feuding with her neighbor. Yet each of these has a special talent and potential, and the caring pastor discovers these, uses them as points of contact, and seeks opportunities for their expression.

Sometimes we meet a person for the first time and feel an immediate negative reaction, but later, as we become well acquainted, we wonder how we could have missed the qualities we have come to appreciate. By making allowances, by always trying to understand, and by caring we can open many doors.

Teach us, we pray, to go beyond liking and disliking to the Christlike ideal of understanding and caring.

COMPENSATIONS

Hast thou entered into the treasures of the snow?
Job 38:22

We live in the mountains where we enjoy much sunshine and frequent winter snowstorms. When the heavy clouds veil the ridges, our friends have varied reactions. Those who have to get to work hope the roads won't be a problem. Our young people, avid skiers who applaud the bumper sticker "Stamp Out Summer," are thrilled with snow and hope for great quantities. A retired friend speaks for many of us who can stay at home when she says, "I'm sorry for the people who will have a hard time driving... but, oh, *isn't it beautiful!*"

A snowy day at home can be a cozy one with a good book, a log on the fire (for those with a hearth), and a neighbor in for coffee. Warm and comfortable, we can stand in our windows looking out on the magic of a transformed world. As the white flakes drifting down cover brown grass, city streets, coating wires and bare branches, I think of the familiar words, "How silently, how silently, the wondrous gift is given." This gift means water in the streams and moisture for all growing things.

It is our privilege to enjoy this beauty without struggling through it, even as we can enjoy grandchildren without the weight of responsibility, pensions without work, and our churches without major responsibility.

Now those of us who like the treasures of the snow have time to watch and say with reverence how beautiful it is.

Whether we spend our years of leisure in the snowy north or the winter-flowering south, may we thank thee for the beauties of thy world, and may we help to preserve them.

TWO SIDES OF THE ROAD

Peace hath her victories, no less renowned than war.
John Milton

We picnicked at Bandelier National Monument in New Mexico one golden September day. The trails were quiet as we walked past big ponderosa pines, through purple aster and crimson paintbrush, while squirrels leaped from branch to branch and the big jays chattered. Around a curve we heard the roar of water and saw the stream dropping sheer for eighty feet, just as it had tumbled for centuries. A clean, refreshing world. But returning to the highway, we faced the ominous steel fences of Los Alamos: DANGER... EXPLOSIVES... KEEP OUT... DANGER... EXPLOSIVES. The signs went on for miles from the strongly guarded entrance.

This is our world today. On one side of the road an effort to conserve natural beauty. On the other the threat of nuclear warfare. Travel across the farm lands of Nebraska in the spring, when roadsides are hung with the the exquisite branches of wild plum, but interspersed are the warning signs, fenced-in areas, and mysterious mounds storing threats of intercontinental destruction. We walk between the beautiful and the terrible.

What can we do? We can become informed and make our opinions known. Age does not wither our voices or our votes. We can act through letters to our congressmen. Through all the turbulence of world affairs today, a quiet voice still speaks to those who listen, "Blessed are the peacemakers."

Help us, each one, to take a stand and to make some contribution to the coming of thy peaceable kingdom.

HARMONY

All people that on earth do dwell,
Sing to the Lord with cheerful voice:
Him serve with fear, His praise forth tell
Come ye before Him and rejoice.
      Genevan Psalter, 1551

As the ushers carried the plates to the chancel to the strains of the Doxology, the woman in the pew ahead gathered up her purse, listened a moment, and then walked out. We began to sing, but this was not the usual "Praise God from Whom all blessings flow," but the Tallis Canon, a more elaborate version with part singing.

The next morning when I was talking to my neighbor, I said I hoped she hadn't felt ill in church. She chuckled a little and explained:

"I don't like that way of singing 'Old Hundred.' Most of us get lost except the choir.

I want the old version that we *can* sing. This has been going on for months now, and I told the minister that the next time I'd walk out—so I had no choice."

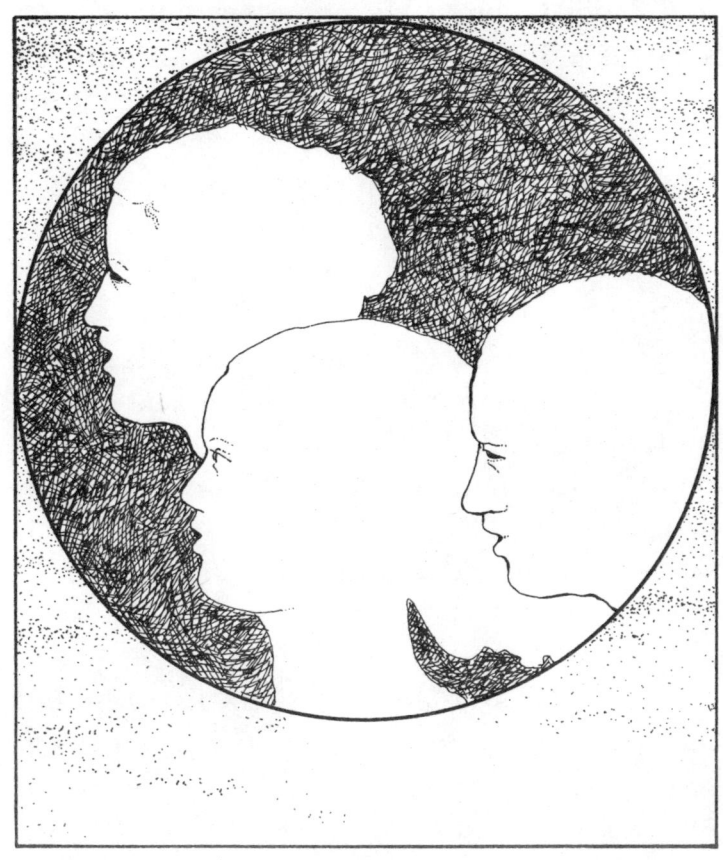

We were amused because we too always foundered. No doubt it was more interesting for our excellent choir, but we missed being able to achieve the final "Praise Father, Son and Holy Ghost!" My friend explained that she was not against change, some innovations were fine, but other forms of worship went too far back and meant too much to change. These would vary from person to person and perhaps from generation to generation.

Worshipers in unfamiliar churches might expect to get lost in the Episcopal Book of Common Prayer or a Catholic Mass, but on our home grounds we expect to be able to participate fully. I think my friend had a valid point. Since there are diversities of gifts, and not all of them musical, there is something to be said for the old version that we all can sing together.

We thank thee for ways of worship that meant much to our ancestors and mean much to us today. Help us as we treasure the old to be open to the new.

THE BOX OF WILTED FLOWERS

I am but one,
But still I am one.
I cannot do everything,
But still I can do something;
And because I cannot do everything
I will not refuse to do the something that I can do.
                              Edward Everett Hale

Every spring the members of our Botanic Gardens rally to work on the annual plant sale which supplies much needed funds for the program of the Gardens. Most of the flowers, herbs, shrubs, and trees are fine, named stock from nurseries, but one popular booth offers home donations at bargain prices. At the last sale one of the workers came in with a dozen boxes of excellent seedlings. Asked about them she explained, "Last year there were some wilted boxes that didn't sell, so I took them home, planted them in my own garden—and look how they multiplied!"

She saw the potential in what might have been tossed out and brought it back increased like the biblical talents. It is the gift of those with imagination to see possibilities and to be concerned enough to make the effort. A backward child can be tutored, a foreign student given hospitality, warm clothes reconditioned for refugees, unsightly grounds made a joy for others to see. And there is a further benefit. Others seeing, for example, the transformation of the box of wilted flowers may exclaim "What a good idea!" and go and do likewise. Imagination, action, influence. From these three can come beautiful results.

We thank thee for those who not only care but act. Help us to find inspiration for ways in which we, too, may serve.

SHARING NOW

You give but little when you give of your possessions. It is when you give of yourself that you truly give.   *Kahlil Gibran*

Sometimes it is possible to give of your possessions and of yourself as well. I think of a woman who taught for many years and has a great love for young people. Although she never married, she has a number of nieces and nephews with families.

"I got to thinking," she told me, "that if I divided up what I have between them in my will, each would get enough for a few tanks of gas, and that would be it. Instead, I bought a little cabin in the mountains, added a room for myself, and invited them to take turns using it for their vacations."

It has been a happy venture. She has had an opportunity to share her love and knowledge of birds, trees, and wildflowers with the children and to come to know them well. Now that it no longer seems wise to spend weeks alone in the mountains, she has company and can make possible vacations for the young families. Someday the oldest nephew will inherit the cabin to use as he sees fit.

Other friends make a point of taking one grandchild at a time on a trip or entertaining each in turn for a weekend. Among our possessions there are apt to be old books, a brooch, a teapot, an antique musket that would be treasured by some of our young relatives. Why not use these as gifts for special occasions and share their enjoyment now? Perhaps we have things that would be of use to church, scouts, or charity organization. Why not share them now? When we use imagination in our giving, we are giving of ourselves with love.

Help us to understand the needs and longings of others and the joy of giving generously.

RETIREMENT INCENTIVES

So teach us to number our days that we may apply our hearts unto wisdom.   Psalm 90:12

Asked how he liked retirement, a well-known clergyman replied, "The only thing I miss is the vacations." When one is working intensively, the weeks of vacation have glamorous appeal. No alarm clock, no fixed schedule, long hours out of doors, leisure to visit, travel to new places. Often people work overtime to complete certain projects with the lure of vacation days ahead. But when the alarm clock is silenced for good, the commuting and long office days over, the permanent vacation may have a different aspect.

We begin to take longer to do simple tasks like raking the lawn, working on income tax, writing that letter. Our former brisk efficiency becomes diluted. Some retirees get deep enjoyment out of their unprogrammed days. Others, like children, running out of things to do at the end of a long summer look forward with excitement (secretly, of course) to the opening of school in September. Such retirees become hungry for something useful and creative to give form to their days. Now is the time to check on extension courses, to learn something new, watch the paper for volunteer appeals, offer special skills to the church, write that long pondered history of the family, resume lapsed hobbies of music, art, or geology, and contribute definite hours to help individuals or organizations. Now that we have time, the challenge is to use it well.

Help us, we pray, to find wisdom in the filling of our days. Through our activities may we grow in understanding and in thy service.

THE CROSS IN THE WORKSHOP

Measure not men by Sundays, without regarding what they do all the week after.
      Thomas Fuller, seventeenth century divine

A young friend was showing me through her new house, a charming place, well suited for the needs of a family with lively children. "And this is my husband's favorite place," she pointed out as we came to a basement workshop. It was obviously a much-used place, but what caught my eye was a small cross made of two rough pieces of wood on the wall above the tools. Their faith meant a great deal to this couple, and the cross above the carpenter's bench was an eloquent reminder, something that surely would be remembered in later years by the children who came in to help or put together their own creations. Because Protestants do not customarily have crosses in their homes, the symbol in this young father's workshop seemed to say that for him, religion was woven deep into the everyday fabric of their lives.

Even if we do not have crosses, religious pictures, or statues in our homes, we can have reminders in other forms. Most of us have treasured books of inspiration, well worn now, that have meant much and helped us. We may have several translations of the Bible, and we may have on our coffee tables recent issues of religious magazines that keep us in touch with news of our denomination and the church at large. We may have recordings of the *Messiah*, the Verdi Requiem, Beethoven's great Ninth Symphony, or familiar hymns. One of my favorites, played each Christmas, is a record of Spanish carols sung at the old Santa Barbara Mission.

Reminders differ according to faith and temperament, but they are helpful in building our religion into a seven-day week.

We pray that that we may live all our days in thy spirit.

WHEN WORRY GNAWS

God grant us serenity to accept the things we cannot change, to change the things we can, and wisdom to know the difference.
Prayer of Alcoholics Anonymous

The problem kept going round and round in her head during the night as though a needle were stuck in a record. There was an ache that had persisted for months. It might be something serious, and this was frightening. But it was frightening, too, to go to a doctor for a definite diagnosis. Although she prayed for health and help, serenity did not seem to come. But the next morning when sunshine banished the dark, suddenly her prayer was answered. The way seemed clear. She would go to the doctor and learn the truth. Worry nourished on uncertainty dropped away, and she knew she could face whatever lay ahead.

When we are troubled in personal relationships, courses of action, distress over the behaviour of others, the conduct of community or national affairs, we can wear ourselves worrying, complaining, lamenting, and making no more progress than a horse on a treadmill. Our choices are two. We can accept or adjust to conditions that are beyond our powers to alter—and do it with good grace. Or we can take definite action, ranging from a possibly painful conversation to writing our congressmen. Either way, fully accepting the hardship for which there is no apparent solution, our action toward a goal will get the needle unstuck, enable us to use our energies constructively and let the music play on.

Help us to face our problems honestly and, with thy guidance, work for their best solution.

A TIME TO SPEAK—AND HOW

A time to keep silence, and a time to speak.
                                        Ecclesiastes 3:7

In the poetry of Ecclesiastes there is a famous passage beginning, "To everything there is a season," and among the listings is "a time to keep silence and a time to speak"— both important to those of us in the years of maturity.

It is difficult to realize how little interest other people, including our children, have in our past lives. The natural impulse of newcomers in our town or church is to refer constantly to what they did, and how they did things, back in Brooklyn or Berkeley. That way of life is often more real than the new environment in which a person may feel unimportant and unrecognized. Hard as it seems, it is wise for the older person to keep silence about the past—except on request or among dear friends with shared memories.

But it is also a time to speak positively. It is a time to show interest in our community, to discuss current issues, to praise what is good. It is a time to ask the opinions of younger people, to seek information about their problems and aspirations. To them the Depression, Pearl Harbor, Lindbergh are part of the dark ages. To establish a bond we must show concern for their concerns. Through this we grow in understanding and in perspective on contemporary thinking. We all have warm memories of certain older people. Weren't they the ones who were genuinely interested in us?

Remembering how Jesus spoke to the individual concerns of his listeners, teach us the wisdom of silence about ourselves but the wisdom of warm and sympathetic words with others.

CARING

We share our mutual woes,
Our mutual burdens bear,
And often for each other flows
The sympathizing tear.

                                    John Fawcett

She went to the hospital to share a long vigil with a friend whose husband was in surgery. Hours can seem unbearably long in a hospital waiting room when the future of one's home and happiness hangs in the balance. At first they visited, talking about all kinds of irrelevant matters. Then the wife, a little embarrassed, said,

"I think I'd like to go into the chapel."

"Let's go together," said her companion. "What good is a friend if she can't pray with you?"

Together they went into the little hospital chapel, and each in her own silence prayed for the patient, for the surgeon, and for needed strength.

Our Catholic neighbors find it much easier to seek such help with no self-consciousness. They find comfort in lighting devotional candles and with these flickering, symbolic gleams shining in the shadows of the church, kneel to repeat their familiar prayers. Many Protestant churches have shown growing interest in groups that join in prayer or pray privately for those in distress. This is a special form of caring, both for the one in pain or trouble and for the lonely one keeping vigil.

We may not actually be able to stand by a friend during the suspense in the waiting room, but we are never too far away for the message, "We are praying for you and with you."

Give us, we pray, the strength and special understanding to share the dark hours of those who need us.

THE PERFECT TRIBUTE

Wisdom resteth in the heart of him that hath understanding.   Proverbs 14:33

We were honoring Miss Jessie at a dinner following our morning service. We think of her as our First Lady because she has been active in our church for seventy years. Her railroad-building father brought her to this Colorado town back in the days of miners, prospectors, and many saloons along the dusty main street. Her career as teacher and principal has given her great understanding of people and a special rapport with the young. She has served on all our boards, taught Sunday school, heartened generations of preachers, and brightened every congregational meeting with common sense opinions spiced with Irish wit.

Miss Jessie is seldom alone in her regular pew on Sunday mornings. A burly football player may tower over her white head, or she may share a hymnbook with a pretty girl or a stray child.

At the dinner tributes were read from former pastors, warm reminiscences contributed by former pupils and present associates. Finally the chairman turned to the guests and asked:

"Would anyone like to add a comment?"

A moment of silence and then a young boy who sometimes sits in her pew, spoke up loud and clear.

"I'd just like to say that Miss Jessie is good company to be in church with."

The crowd applauded. He had spoken for all of us. This is something to think about . . . Are *we* good company to be in church with?

We thank thee for those bright spirits whose joy is in service, whose warm interest flows unfailingly to others. Help us to grow in our capacity to befriend others of all ages, especially the lonely and the stranger.

HAVE A GOOD DAY

Sing unto the Lord a new song   Psalm 149:1

As I walked down the steps of our library a young couple who had been talking together bicycled off in opposite directions, and I caught the words tossed over the boy's shoulder, "Have a good day, and I love you, too."

Have a good day or a nice day. This is the expression we hear across the country, in restaurants, gas stations, stores, and between friends. In some areas it's "You have a good day, folks," a pleasant salutation, less formal than the old "good morning," more meaningful than "hi," if not as beautiful as the Spanish "Go with God."

What makes a good day? While it's different for different people, here are some suggestions.

A little work to give structure to the day and to give us a sense of worth.

A little play, because we are pleasanter people if we keep the habit of enjoyment through visits, games, outdoor recreation, and shared laughter.

A little outreach to someone beyond the immediate circle in the form of a letter, remembrance, or volunteer service.

A little growth through learning something new or improving our skills.

A little prayer—or more than a little—for guidance and understanding on this day.

If our days are rich in meaning we may not toss the words over our shoulders, but our attitude will say to others, "Have a nice day, and I love you, too."

May we live this day well, reflecting the joy of thy love in our words and our actions.

TREES WITHOUT LEAVES

The woods, divested in great part of their leaves, are being ventilated. It is the season of perfect works, of hard tough, ripe twigs, not of tender buds and leaves . . . It is only the perennial that you see, the iron age of the year.   Henry David Thoreau

When we think of beautiful trees we usually picture leafy boughs giving shade, whispering in the wind, glimmering satin green or silver, alive with birds darting into their shelter. In winter a greater view opens. Now we see the structure, where limbs have grown from the trunk, how branches have been bent by storms, scars of old battles with the wind, but with the promise of renewed life in the buds already formed at the tip of each twig. Most children would only see beauty in the summer tree, but as we grow older we

learn more about the structure of life. We know that deep roots make both strong trees and strong men. We know that great stresses can be sustained and, even if scars remain, recovery is possible. Because we have more understanding of motives, frustrations, and longings, we can look beyond outward appearance to character.

Black trees in delicate etching against the snow. Is this a cold, forbidding sight? For those who can see it, there is great beauty, for here is character laid bare. And just as we can marvel at this saga of growth, survival, and aspiration, so, with mature eyes, we can see the beauty of a human soul grown strong through struggle, courage, and faith.

Give us, we pray, perception to look past forbidding exteriors to find the beauty and strength in human character.

THANKSGIVING

*Now thank we all our God
With heart and hands and voices.*
                    Martin Rinkart, c. 1636

On Thanksgiving eve in our church we had a family service, marked with an unaccustomed obligato of little chirps and cheerful squirming. The minister came down from the chancel and, standing close to the congregation, called for an "impromptu litany." Individuals were asked to participate by saying "I am thankful for" with a response from the others, "We give thanks to the Lord." After a few adults spoke, the children caught the idea. A four year old in front of us, cuddling her doll, said, just above a whisper, "I'm thankful for my Raggedy Ann." A slightly older boy declared with conviction, "I'm thankful for food." Then in a man's voice, strong and quiet, from somewhere behind us, came the words, "I'm thankful for life and all it offers."

It was a spacious thought, going beyond gratitude for such specifics as home, church, work, and family, because it included our opportunity to make something of what we have. His gratitude was not finite, but open-ended. Some of the things life would offer might be difficult and sorrowful, but with faith there would be values in all of life's experiences.

When we are young and vigorous, the world is full of possibilities for career, adventure, friendship, home, and family. When limitations develop in strength, income, loss of loved ones, and perhaps separateness of grown children, there are still many factors we can control through our attitudes. Now it is helpful to be thankful for the wonderful gift of life—AND ALL IT STILL OFFERS.

We thank thee for the meaning faith gives life and for the opportunity each day offers to try to live in the spirit of thy Son.

THE QUIET MOMENTS OF CHRISTMAS

As with gladness men of old did the guiding star behold . . .
So, most Gracious God, may we evermore be led to Thee.   *William C. Dix*

Christmas comes around very quickly at this stage of life, and we hear a good many sighs and weary comments such as "I'm getting pretty tired of all this rush . . . too much commercialism . . . floods of breakable toys for the children . . . rising expectations . . . not the way it was when we were young . . ."

Granted that the birth of Jesus has little connection with bargains in color TV or gorgeous packages of liquor, there are other aspects that hold their old beauty. I think of these as the quiet moments of Christmas, and for each person they are different. I remember as a small child a supernumerary angel in a pageant suddenly being struck with the beauty of "Silent Night." I remember a Christmas Eve when our own children were small. The tree was trimmed, gifts piled under it, and the rest of the family asleep. I sat alone enjoying the colored lights with a wonderful feeling of peace—and waiting. Again, walking alone on a snowy village street, I turned the corner and there was our church, its Christmas lights shining in the darkness. It, too, seemed to be waiting.

We can't go back to the treasured experiences of our younger days, but our Christmas can still have special meaning. We can remember in some way or visit those who might be forgotten. We can enjoy the eager-faced children at the Christmas Eve family service or the young people, often hand in hand, who attend the midnight service. We can listen to our favorite music, and, going back to the source, read again or listen again to the story of the nativity. Perhaps in these quiet moments we will know once more the

old sense of excitement when we hear the words, "and there were in the same country shepherds abiding in the field keeping watch."

Grant, we pray, that the coming of the Christ Child may be the focus of our Christmas, and may we honor him by showing our love for others.

BREAKING NEW GROUND
—A Thought for the New Year

Sow to yourselves in righteousness, reap in mercy; break your fallow ground: for it is time to seek the Lord, till he come and rain righteousness upon you.
                                                                Hosea 10:12

The oldest church in Nottingham, England, has a tall steeple that reaches high above the statue of Robin Hood across the street and up toward the site of the castle on the hill, once the stronghold of his adversary, the sheriff. It is an impressive steeple with a big clock, but there is something unique about this clock. Circling its face in bright gold letters between the numerals is the message: It Is Time to Seek the Lord. An appropriate message for a church clock, surely, but it puzzled me until I found it in the prophecy of Hosea.

Here it is more than a reminder. It is a

stern admonition imbedded in a book of dire reproaches for evil and threat of punishment. While few passersby would realize its source, the seven words are eloquent in themselves. No special hour, such as 11 A.M. Sunday morning, is indicated as the time to serve the Lord. As the hands sweep around, all the hours of the day are included.

The meaning is richer, too, when we think of the context—break your fallow ground. We should look to our unused and dormant resources. How do we go about this? We look for new ways to serve, and we are sensitive to situations where we may help.

Modern architects are not putting many clocks in towers these days and, indeed, are building few steeples, but I like to remember the church in Nottingham with the message spelled out so clearly for passersby on their way to work: This is the time!

Help us to serve thee not only by tending our accustomed fields, but by breaking our fallow ground for a greater harvest.

ENLARGE OUR LOVE

Beareth all things, believeth all things, hopeth all things.   I Cor. 13:7

In New York City, where school tensions often become violent, a gentle young black woman who deals in human relations has a motto on her wall which says that "there is no door that enough love will not open."

Her work involves many crises of racism, strikes, and outbreaks that can flare into dangerous proportions, but she always strives for understanding, not only of the immediate situation but of the hidden cause. Often this has led to improvement.

Some doors that we encounter seem not only closed but bolted. There are difficult personalities who seem hostile and resentful. It takes a special kind of love to get past their defenses—not just an effusive outpouring of goodwill. A rebellious young person may flout his parents because he lacks self confidence; a thorny fellow worker may be jealous; a cantankerous older person may be pitifully lonely.

When our love is large enough to reach beyond personal offense, it can offer real comfort, as all of us know who have handled small children. "I won't!" storms the child to his mother, "and I hate you." She listens unruffled. "You know what, Johnny? I think you're hungry. Let's have some milk and crackers." Continuing to storm, he follows his mother to the kitchen and minutes later is sharing a snack happily, the sun shining again. It takes love that overrides the personal to help open the closed doors.

Enlarge our capacity for loving, we pray, that we may ever grow in our understanding of Christ's teaching to love one another.

THE TIME IS NOW

I shall pass through this world but once. If, therefore, there be any kindness I can show, or any good thing I can do, let me do it now, let me not defer it or neglect it, for I shall not pass this way again.

These familiar words, in circulation for more than a century, have been attributed, uncertainly, to Emerson, Carlyle, Wesley, two Quakers (Stephen Grellet and William Penn), and several others. This simple message, serving as both reminder and inspiration, has been quoted, reprinted on cards, and framed on walls in ways that surely would have amazed its originator.

What he does not go on to say is that kindness often breeds kindness and good deeds inspire other good deeds. The alcoholic who has been helped through Alcoholics Anonymous helps others. A man, remember-

> I shall pass through this world but once
> If, therefore, there be any kindness
> I can show, or any good thing I can do,
> let me do it now,
> let me not defer it or neglect it
> for I shall not pass this way again

ing how important financial help was to his education, gives money for scholarships. A woman, appreciating a friendly welcome in the loneliness of a new location, offers her services to a newcomers' club. A person who has experienced the concern of others who remember him, not just in the immediate crisis of grief, but in the empty months that come later, may repeat this thoughtful follow-up.

When we, remembering special influences and encouragement at critical times in our lives, do our best to pass these on, who knows how far they may go? A simple deed of kindness need not be a one-time incident, but like windborn seed, may alight to root, flower, and send forth seeds again.

In our years of maturity, when outside obligations are reduced and our understanding deepened by years of working, struggling, suffering, enjoying, and loving, we are especially equipped to make a practice of showing kindness and doing whatever good things are within our power. The time is now!

We thank thee for the words and actions of Christ, remembered for two thousand years and still inspiring men and women to help, to comfort and to care. May we, now in our years of maturity, be so inspired.